Acting Edition

This Is NOT a Teen Movie

BY **Jane B. Jones**

FOR PRODUCTION INQUIRIES
UNITED STATES AND CANADA
info@concordtheatricals.com
1-866-979-0447
UNITED KINGDOM AND EUROPE
licensing@concordtheatricals.co.uk
020-7054-7298

Each title is subject to availability from Concord Theatricals Corp., depending upon country of performance. Please be aware that *THIS IS NOT A TEEN MOVIE* may not be licensed by Concord Theatricals Corp. in your territory. Professional and amateur producers should contact the nearest Concord Theatricals Corp. office or licensing partner to verify availability.

No one shall make any changes in this title(s) for the purpose of production. No part of this book may be reproduced, stored in a retrieval system, scanned, uploaded, or transmitted in any form, by any means, now known or yet to be invented, including mechanical, electronic, digital, photocopying, recording, videotaping, or otherwise, without the prior written permission of the publisher. No one shall share this title(s), or any part of this title(s), through any social media or file hosting websites.

For all inquiries regarding motion picture, television, online/digital and other media rights, please contact Concord Theatricals Corp.

MUSIC AND THIRD-PARTY MATERIALS USE NOTE

Licensees are solely responsible for obtaining formal written permission from copyright owners to use copyrighted music and/or other copyrighted third-party materials (e.g. artworks, logos) in the performance of this play and are strongly cautioned to do so. If no such permission is obtained by the licensee, then the licensee must use only original music and materials that the licensee owns and controls. Licensees are solely responsible and liable for clearances of all third-party copyrighted materials, including without limitation music, and shall indemnify the copyright owners of the play(s) and their licensing agent, Concord Theatricals Corp., against any costs, expenses, losses and liabilities arising from the use of such copyrighted third-party materials by licensees. For music, please contact the appropriate music licensing authority in your territory for the rights to any incidental music.

IMPORTANT BILLING AND CREDIT REQUIREMENTS

If you have obtained performance rights to this title, please refer to your licensing agreement for important billing and credit requirements.

This Is NOT a Teen Movie was first performed by the Youth Performing Arts School in Louisville, Kentucky, on September 19, 2024. It was directed by Jane B. Jones with dramaturgy by Amy Wegener. The production team was Cayce Abellard, Amy Berry, Jen Groseth, and Alan Perez, and the stage managers were Samantha Burch and Soleil Merwarth. The cast was as follows:

REINA . . . . Layla Sanders
TRENT . . . . Charley Ignatow
STEPH . . . . Nadia Linton
ADAM . . . . Dante Baisas
EM . . . . Andy Wallace
JACYLN . . . . Rahini Allen
ETHAN . . . . Maxton Fee
DR. GRAY . . . . Grayson Beverly
KRIS . . . . Corrine Gannott
KAYLA . . . . Kate Michael Stewart
MICHELLE . . . . Maya Williamson
BRITTANY . . . . Abigail Herrensmith
TERRY . . . . Kode Embers
JIMMY . . . . Daniel Gonzalez
ALEX . . . . Giani Roberts
DYLAN . . . . Jack Masterson
ENSEMBLE . . . . Joselin Dominguez, Timyah Hall,
Violet Henderson, Elijah Hutchison, Willow Fox Young

CHARACTERS

REINA – High school senior, alt-nerd (the kind who alternates between loving school and wishing she was already in college where her life will finally begin), female, Black or mixed

TRENT – High school senior, alt-nerd (very invested in being the cool, smart one), slightly codependent with Reina, nonbinary

STEPH – High school senior, quietly smart and fun and funny and just trying to get through without becoming internet infamous, female

ADAM – High school senior, dabbles in a little bit of everything – e.g. runs track and does the school play, male

EM – High school senior, cool loner type (who definitely volunteers at Planned Parenthood and is a little judgy about people who aren't as committed to the cause as they are), nonbinary

JACYLN BALDWIN – New principal, Reina's mother, just got the promotion she's been working toward for years and yet gets the short end of the stick at the same time i.e. the story of her whole damn life, fifties, female, Black or mixed

ETHAN – College freshman, entitled and oblivious, not evil but also totally wrecked by social expectation, male, white

DR. GRAY – Dean of Residence Life, wants to help teens become adults and is terrified of what could happen if they don't, any gender

KRIS – *Golden Apple* reporter, any gender

KAYLA – Model UN or similar club, holds a low-level position in student government, doesn't want anyone to look at her, female

MICHELLE – Quiz bowl or similar club, sings in the school choir, is ready to lead, female

BRITTANY – Great at chemistry, family moves a lot, hasn't quite settled into a friend group, female

TERRY – Plays an individual sport like track, tennis, or archery; never raises his hand in class; male

JIMMY – On the soccer team with Adam; got a great SAT or ACT score but hasn't told anyone, including his parents; male

ALEX – A bro's bro, watches sports and plays video games and is coasting along, male

DYLAN – Was told he was hot once in middle school and has since had the inflated ego of a hot middle schooler, male

ENSEMBLE – Six to eight other students

SETTING

Golden Valley High,
a high school out of a teen movie, too slick, too rich, the cool students
are clearly models and the athletes are all training for the Olympics.
And also just a high school.

AUTHOR'S NOTES

As language and references change quickly, please feel free to update slang
and references to specific works of art, technology, or memes to fit your
production. Additionally, there is the opportunity to make jokes unique
to your audience. For example, Ms. William's AP Lang class was voted the
hardest class by the cast, and Prime sponsored our archery team.

I've limited the cursing, but if you need to make further adjustments,
please omit rather than replace with words like "dang."

Scene 1: Promposals

(A high school cafetorium, three lunch tables.)

(A projection or smart board shows slides promoting school events.)

*(A **GIRL** comes on and cycles through the signs until landing on the last one [Archery Scores Bull's-eye with New Sponsor, Join Robotics Club: Build the Future, Auditions* for Cinderella *and* Death of a Salesman *This Friday in the Drama Room, Announcing the Prom Theme: Hollywood Royalty].)*

*(Two **BOYS** appear on opposite sides of the stage. They have promposal supplies [poster board with some cute "Will you go to prom with me?" line and flowers or balloons]. They spot the **GIRL**. She tries to sneak away, but realizes she's flanked. The **BOYS** see each other and rush to get to her first. One **BOY** trips; the other gets to her. She pretends delight, and she reluctantly agrees to go to prom. [This can be mimed or ad-libbed.] **BOY** drapes his arm over her shoulders, takes a picture, and leads **GIRL** off. The other **BOY** looks dejected then spots another **GIRL** and runs off after her.)*

*(A crowd of **PROMPOSERS** runs across the stage. It's a herd of bouquets, balloons, streamers, and poster boards or banners with cute messages. The various student groups cross the stage, excited about prom! Feel free to throw in some teen-movie references – guy runs past with boom*

box over his head, Molly Ringwald look-alike in pink dances through pursued by nerd, or whatever will be recognizable to your audience.)

(Yes, there is definitely music under all this: upbeat and poppy, but also a bit off. [Like how all those "I love you so much I'm stalking you" songs just aren't cute anymore.])*

*(**REINA** is revealed as the crowd thins onstage with a notebook and pen. As someone runs past with a balloon or streamer, she pops the balloon and a small amount of confetti bursts from the balloon or she snags a streamer.)*

REINA. Dear Diary, aka journal for my therapist to uncover the root of my teenage angst aka work I'm doing now so I don't wake up middle-aged and miserable – if I make it to fifty with all the global crises, ohmygod, what if the life expectancy drops and I'm already middle-aged?! Whoa, stop, stop! –

The immediate issue is it's prom season and I *HATE* it. Yeah, yeah, nerdy weirdo hates the big dance, big deal, we've seen it.

Except I actually *LOVE* it.

I've seen all the movies, and I know it's a lie, but I want the teen-movie prom soo bad!
The dress, the corsage.
The beautiful and tastefully themed decor.
The devastatingly attractive, but also thoughtful and witty date.

---

* A license to produce *THIS IS NOT A TEEN MOVIE* does not include a performance license for any third-party or copyrighted music. Licensees should create an original composition or use music in the public domain. For further information, please see the Music and Third-Party Materials Use Note on page iii.

And it all begins with a big romantic gesture that is waaay too public but also sweet and genuine that sweeps you off your feet aka the Promposal.

If you remember the trends of flash mobs, sky writing, surprise wedding proposals, it's like that, but for prom, because teenagers can commit to cringe romance waaay better than adults.

Unfortunately, around here promposals are low-key aggressive. Some of these guys break up with their girlfriends over winter break just so they can spend the spring semester hunting for the perfect prom date.

I know that sounds dramatic, but that's because it *is*!

OK, Reina, suck it up, life isn't a movie. Just *don't* go to prom – problem solved.

But why should I stay home just because they suck all the fun out it?

(**TRENT** *enters.*)

TRENT. You're glowering again.

REINA. What?

TRENT. Staring, menacingly, like you mean to do someone harm.

REINA. That's just my thinking face.

TRENT. Are you plotting to tear down the patriarchy again?

REINA. Always!

TRENT. Great, because I have some words about the way Mr. Harrison is characterizing the role of women in World War II, it's like the man is stuck in the history he teaches. That's good! Do you think your mom would like that? Reina? Reina? Are you listening to me?

REINA. (*Looking away, distracted.*) Yeah, yeah. Mr. Harrison, misogyny or something...

TRENT. Are you like, trying to stay neutral and not use your new position of power and influence 'cause your mom's the new principal?

REINA. That would be very evolved of me, but no.

Promposals have started and it's all just so – ugh!

(**STEPH** *and* **ADAM** *enter.*)

STEPH. I know that look, war? Starvation? AP History test?

TRENT. Promposals.

STEPH. Ooohhh.

REINA. Isn't it too soon?!

It's too soon.

ADAM. Come on, you'd totally swoon if someone jumped out of a cake for you.

REINA. A cake?

ADAM. Dylan did that during first lunch.

STEPH. Who did he ask?

ADAM. The transfer, Brittany, he sits next to her in Chem.

REINA. Oh, OK, so I guess that means he values her brain as well as her gorgeous hair?

STEPH. What flavor?

ADAM. It wasn't a real cake, Steph, it was a prop from the theatre department.

STEPH. So she didn't get any cake?

TRENT. Poor Brittany, locked in to going to prom with Dylan Morris. He's going to spend the whole night making her dance too close and trying to explain the plot of *Oppenheimer.*

REINA. And she didn't even get any actual cake!

ADAM. I thought you feminists would be on board for guys bending over backward for girls' attention and approval?

REINA. I'm all for gender-role reversals, but it just feels like all these stunts are a competition between guys. It's like the girl doesn't even matter as soon as she says yes.

ADAM. I mean you're not gonna say no after he goes through all that effort?

STEPH. Not while everyone's filming, that would be so embarrassing.

REINA. Exactly!

So even if you don't really like the guy, you can't say NO! Because he did this big, performative thing to like WIN you.

ADAM. You're just bitter 'cause no one's going to prompose to you.

> (**EM** *walks over to their table with a small handful of flyers.*)

EM. Hey Reina.

REINA. Hey... Em.

How've you been since math?!

EM. Last period?

REINA. Whew! Yeah, that test, huh?! Glad we're done with that!

EM. I guess.

You're good at math, you're always right when Ms. Barrett calls on you.

REINA. You noticed that?

EM. Yeah. Math isn't really my thing.

REINA. Oh! Well, maybe we should study together?

EM. Yeah. Cool. So, I'll just message you.

REINA. Yeah. Cool. Message me...about math.

EM. Yeah.

REINA. Yeah.

> *(A pause. They just look at each other for a bit;
> its awkward, but cute.)*

TRENT. Okaayy, bye!

EM. Um actually, *Trent – (Going into their prepared
speech.)* I – I'm a peer educator for the clinic downtown.

TRENT. Uh-huh, we know. You bring it up all the time.

EM. *Anyway*, we're having a teach-in about how to report
assault and like what questions to expect and how to
collect evidence so you can make your case.

STEPH. God, that sounds awful.

EM. Yeah, it totally is, we just want people to be prepared,
you know?

REINA. Yeah, yeah, I get it.

ADAM. Wouldn't it be better to teach people not to get
assaulted? Like how to be safe?

TRENT. I think you mean it would be better to teach
people *not* to assault each other.

ADAM. Same thing.

STEPH. No, it's not.

EM. Yeah, we're into prevention too, of course, this won't
be the only teach-in...

REINA. Yeah, one step at a time, right?

EM. Yeah, so if you're interested...

> *(**EM** starts to hand **REINA** a flyer; **TRENT** takes
> it.)*

TRENT. Got it. Thanks!

> (**EM** *starts to go;* **REINA** *takes the flyer from* **TRENT.**)

REINA. Thanks! See you in math!

EM. Yeah, OK, see you, bye.

> (**EM** *exits.* **REINA** *watches them go.* **TRENT** *watches* **REINA.**)

STEPH. Don't you think it's safer not to get asked to prom?

ADAM. Safer?

REINA. Maybe.

STEPH. Being alone in the car with some guy, it just freaks me out.

ADAM. Guy, right here!

REINA. You don't count, we know you.

ADAM. You know all the guys here. We've been in school together for years.

STEPH. My sister was friends with *Ethan*, the guy that got kicked out of U of C for, you know, assault. She thought she knew him.

TRENT. Damn.

ADAM. That's different.

REINA. How?

ADAM. It's college. They were probably partying.

REINA. Are you really trying to tell me people don't "party" on prom night?

ADAM. Well, no – but – where would you even do it? I can't bring anyone over without my parents knowing.

STEPH. Not everyone's parents are like yours.

ADAM. Nobody's parents would just *let* their son do that.

REINA. How many people, how many *parents*, do you know that said "Oh Ethan, he was a good boy, he would never do anything like that." How many people came to his defense and called her a slut?

STEPH. My parents! They were like, well, there's two sides to every story. How do you think that makes me feel? What if something like that happened to me, could I tell them?

REINA. You could always come to me. To my mom.

STEPH. Yeah, I know, it just sucks, you know?

TRENT. Yeah.

Reina, would your mom? Could she like, cancel prom?

REINA. Oh, there'll be a prom. The PTA would rampage if she tried to cancel it.

ADAM. So you're going?

REINA. Maybe.

ADAM. Hypocrite! You talk about guys like we're all creeps, but you just want someone to sweep you off your feet like some *Twilight* sparkly vampire bullshit.

REINA. That's so reductive, my actual feels are much more nuanced. And I'm Team Jacob anyway.

> (*The bell rings.* **ADAM** *exits.* **REINA** *lingers;* **TRENT** *and* **STEPH** *realize* **REINA** *isn't leaving with them.*)

TRENT. This better be worth Ms. Weimer's lecture on punctuality.

REINA. Adam is such a...knob!

TRENT. We don't have to stay friends with him after we graduate.

REINA. It's just...he's right!

I want someone to take my glasses off and let down my ponytail and tell me I'm pretty.

TRENT. You don't wear glasses.*   **STEPH.** Ponytail?

REINA. You guuyys! You know what I mean!

STEPH. Sorry, sorry, we do!

TRENT. Of course, we do.

REINA. I can't believe I've bought into this mass-marketed fantasy! Why am I so pathetic?!

TRENT.   **STEPH.**
   Don't talk to my friend like that!   Sandwich time!

REINA. No therapy tools!

TRENT. You are smart, creative, and passionate.

STEPH. You're always teaching me about injustice and how we can make a difference in the world.

   But ALL your comfort media –

TRENT. Books, movies, TV shows, podcasts, Reddit threads, Pinterest boards –

   Center around unrealistic teen romance.

REINA. OK, OK, I get it.

STEPH. And you're so caring and idealistic –

TRENT. And thoughtful and funny.

   (**TRENT** *and* **STEPH** *group hug* **REINA.**)

TRENT & STEPH. And we love, love, LOVE you!

TRENT. Let's go as a platonic triad!

STEPH. Yes! Like SpongeBob, Patrick, and Squidward.

REINA. Ummm...

TRENT. I can style our outfits!

* OR: You can't see anything without your glasses.

STEPH. I preemptively veto the latest avant-garde drag trend!

TRENT. Fair, fair. My Chappell Roan Goth Baby drag was strong – but wrong.

STEPH. The concept was brilliant, the actual outfit just needed some...editing.

TRENT. Classically stylish with a modern flair?

REINA. I guess...   **STEPH.** YES!

TRENT. I can see it in my mind already! This is going to be so fun!

> *(The late bell rings.* **TRENT** *and* **STEPH** *hurry off.)*

> *(***REINA*** speaks to the audience.)*

REINA. That *is* the "right" answer.
Go with your friends – Just like every other dance, party, and event for all of high school.
We'll make the same jokes and eat at our favorite diner, and it will all be the same.

But...
It's PROM! Senior PROM!
It should be special,
twinkling lights, swelling music, a real date at a nice restaurant – slow dancing, heart pounding in your ears – maybe even.

> *(She mimes a kiss.)*

And it starts with a promposal, not a compliment sandwich.
No, no!
Just do the right thing.
Just do what you always do.
You already agreed, sort of, basically...

You didn't say yes, but nobody really asked, it's just implied...

(**STEPH** *pops back onstage.*)

STEPH. Reina, come on we've got to get to class! Someone's going to tell your mom that you skipped English.

Scene 2: Hardball with the Principal

(Lights shift to highlight a different section of the cafetorium; the projection has a "Welcome New Principal Baldwin" slide. **PRINCIPAL BALDWIN** *enters as if to cut through on her way to something important and is interrupted by* **KRIS**.*)*

KRIS. Principal Baldwin? Hi, I'm Kris with *The Golden Apple*, you said I could come by to get a statement for our next issue?

JACYLN. Yes, always happy to support the student newspaper.

KRIS. Is it true that the culture at this high school promotes or even creates sexual predators?

JACYLN. I – um. I was not aware that that's what you were writing about. You said an article about current events – I thought the new dress code –

KRIS. Six alums from last year's graduating class have been suspended from their colleges.

JACYLN. Six? I'd only heard about – no I guess with that boy from U of C that's…

KRIS. With three more under investigation.

JACYLN. More! How do you know that?

KRIS. Social media.

   We actually have a really strong alumni network, word travels fast.

JACYLN. Well, I suppose that's a silver lining –

KRIS. So, do you think it's true that our school culture promotes sexually predatory behavior?

JACYLN. No!

KRIS. No? Is that your full statement?

JACYLN. No.

I –

I don't think it's the culture of our school, specifically. But more of a societal issue...with lots of factors –

KRIS. Then why are there so many incidents with recent graduates from this school specifically?

JACYLN. Um, well, we are a large school... With a robust athletic program –

KRIS. You're saying sports promote aggressive behavior and hypermasculinity?

JACYLN. No, I – where did you learn those words?

KRIS. Social media.

There's a lot of really great information mixed in with the brain rot.

JACYLN. It could be that more people are coming forward because there's less stigma around being victimized and more faith that the system will hold people accountable.

KRIS. So, it's a good thing these students are getting kicked out of school?

JACYLN. It's a good thing the schools are investigating the allegations and issuing appropriate consequences once the students are determined to be culpable.

KRIS. But you have to admit it looks really bad for us. Six from Golden Valley in one year, that's more abusers than a starting lineup of basketball players.

JACYLN. While the actions of alumni may influence how people see Golden Valley High, that does not change our mission to provide all students with a quality education.

KRIS. So you're not going to do anything? Is that what you're saying?

JACYLN. As the new principal, I'll need to speak to the PTA and school admin team, and we'll find an appropriate way to address people's concerns.

KRIS. Are you aware we don't have a sexual harassment policy?

The teachers do, but not student to student.

JACYLN. It falls under the anti-bullying policy.

KRIS. They don't talk about it in that video we have to watch every year, the one with flip phones and dancing emojis that nobody takes seriously.

JACYLN. Kris, I should be getting on with –

*(She starts to usher **KRIS** out.)*

KRIS. I know you're new and all, and I probably shouldn't say, but the vibe around here isn't good. Girls are looking around like "Am I next?" And some of them, the guys from the reports, I'm like surprised, but not surprised. But Ethan, he was, well I *thought* he was a nice guy. He knew my name, I interviewed him once after a game and he remembered my name and he would say hi to me in the hallway. And, now I keep thinking, like, should I have known?

JACYLN. How could you?

KRIS. I dunno. But it feels like somebody should have.

JACYLN. We can't always anticipate how people will behave.

KRIS. Sure.

Anyway, I really do hope you find a way of "addressing people's concerns."

JACYLN. We will.

KRIS. Because people think you won't.

JACYLN. Why?

KRIS. Nobody else did.

JACYLN. We'll address it. You can quote me.

KRIS. OK, thanks Principal Baldwin. Have a good day.

JACYLN. You too, Kris.

Scene 3: Restorative Process

(A portion of the cafetorium is transformed into a small office; the projection has a U of C slide. **DR. GRAY** *is at their desk.* **ETHAN** *enters.)*

DR. GRAY. Ethan, thank you for coming today. If this goes well, it could be a model –

ETHAN. Coach said if I do community service or fines or whatever, I can come back to practice.

DR. GRAY. That's not entirely true. You're on probation. This semester, you'll finish your work remotely and *if* you take responsibility for your actions, you can return to campus next fall.

ETHAN. Next FALL! You can't do that! I'm an athlete, I have to go to practice. I was *recruited* to be here!

DR. GRAY. Consider that that may be why you aren't expelled.

Before you return, you'll need to make a public apology.

ETHAN. Hell no. I'm not weak.

DR. GRAY. The public nature of your transgression drew a lot of attention. Some people are emulating your behavior; there's been an increase of derogatory and threatening comments to female students and staff in person and online.

ETHAN. Emu-what?

DR. GRAY. Emulate – imitate, copy.

ETHAN. That sounds kinda like...

DR. GRAY. Emasculate?

ETHAN. yeah.

DR. GRAY. You don't like that word.

ETHAN. It's just a word.

DR. GRAY. Words matter. Do you understand that your words as much as your actions toward Lindsey led to your removal from campus?

ETHAN. Ohh, I get it. You're on *her* side.

DR. GRAY. I'm on the college's side. As the Dean of Residence Life, it's my job to ensure that this campus is a safe place for *everyone*. You're all here to learn, get your degrees, and move on with your lives. I want that for you! The problem is, your actions have made people on this campus, especially women, feel *unsafe*, and people cannot learn when they feel afraid.

We're trying to work within a restorative model – I'm here to help you make amends and repair the harm you caused.

ETHAN. I'm not the problem here, it's her! When I was in high school, everybody loved me. And the girls didn't pull any of this hot-and-cold shit.

DR. GRAY. OK, you got along with girls during high school. Great! Let's start there. Who was your last girlfriend?

ETHAN. Lauren Halter.

DR. GRAY. What was she like?

ETHAN. hot.

DR. GRAY. And?

ETHAN. What?

DR. GRAY. What made her your girlfriend?

ETHAN. We fooled around.

DR. GRAY. Did you meet her parents, or go places together, or have any shared interests?

ETHAN. *(Ticking the questions off on his fingers.)* No, my house, fooling around.

DR. GRAY. Did she like fooling around?

ETHAN. She never complained.

DR. GRAY. Did you ever ask her directly?

ETHAN. Why would I?

DR. GRAY. How long was your relationship?

ETHAN. I dunno, a month? We starting going out 'cause I asked her to prom. *(Gets into telling this story.)* I saw this thing online where a guy surprised a girl with a dorky sign and some flowers and was like, I can do better than that! I got her a bunch of balloons and did a backflip off her porch.

That's how it is now at my school, you've got to go all out. I guess people have always wanted to emu– act like me.

DR. GRAY. Do any of the girls ever say no?

ETHAN. They're not blue-ball witches.

DR. GRAY. If they did say no, is that what they would be?

ETHAN. That's a dumb question.

DR. GRAY. Do you know when you stopped seeing girls, women, as people?

ETHAN. What?

> *(Promposal transition: A promposal of your choice, should be overly intense in some way.)*

> *(From the first production [inspired by a real promposal]:* **GIRL** *walks across stage and* **BOY** *in police hat calls out –*

> **BOY.** Stop! Freeze! Say yes or you're under arrest.

> **GIRL.** Yes?

> *They walk off with his arm around her shoulder; she seems shell-shocked.)*

Scene 4: What Do They Want?

(The cafetorium a week later. Projection: "Prom Tickets on Sale: Walk the Red Carpet." **MICHELLE** *and* **KAYLA** *enter with their lunches.)*

MICHELLE. Davon, Jeremy, and Dylan Morris are already booked.

I guess it's a bummer about Davon, he has leadership potential, but Jeremy only got a twenty-three on the ACT and Dylan seems like a closet psycho.

KAYLA. Do we really have to do this?

MICHELLE. Don't do that thing where you downplay a big moment – this is not going to be like your sixteenth birthday where have another sleepover just us because you don't want people to think you're a pick-me.

KAYLA. But we had so much fun, just the two of us.

Quiet, at-home fun.

MICHELLE. I will do this without you.

...

Pleeeeease don't make me do this without you.

KAYLA. Fine.

Who are they going with?

MICHELLE. Davon's going with Anna B.

Basically dating, so – cute.

Jeremy asked Hazel. Which is frankly cradle robbing! She's only a sophomore!

But it'll be a big boost for her. She'll probably get to go to three proms!

KAYLA. It's still sketchy. And three proms? That's a lot of money.

MICHELLE. Who cares! Prom is our night to be princesses! Princesses don't care about money!

KAYLA. Princesses only exist in the world of landed gentry and Disneyland. We beggars have to save for college. *(À la Oliver.)* Please sir, can I have a higher education?

MICHELLE. Shh! Shh! Shh! There is no money on prom night. There are only beautiful dresses, perfectly coiffed hair, non-allergy-inducing flower arrangements, and handsome, tastefully matching dates. And a horse-drawn carriage that takes you to the entrance of the ball.

KAYLA. A carriage?!

MICHELLE. Don't dis my vision, I'm manifesting!

KAYLA. I just don't want *everyone* to look at me.

Can't we be like undercover princesses?

MICHELLE. All other details are negotiable, but first we must get the right dates!

(Dropping a bomb.) Dylan Morris asked Brittany.

KAYLA. Noooo! She's so pretty, she could go with anyone! Dylan is literally an idiot! He only wants to go to college so he can be in a frat. I bet he secretly practices keg stands and flip cup instead of studying!

MICHELLE. He was smart enough to swoop up Brittany, so maybe he's not a complete bonehead? Anyway, at least that means he won't be asking one of us. I want to be able to look back at these pictures without having to repress any memories.

KAYLA. My mom always tells me how magical her prom was, but it doesn't add up, 'cause I know she went with her high school boyfriend and all the other stories she tells about him make him seem like a real sleaze.

How about Tim and Kamari from Model UN?

MICHELLE. They are so boring! All they care about is physics, diplomatic relations, and writing AO3 fan fiction.

KAYLA. Boring isn't always bad. I had a class with that guy Ethan.

MICHELLE. What? When?

KAYLA. Freshman year when we had different maths. He seemed nice. Not the brightest, but he always smiled at me when I walked in and asked me to help him with the problem sets a couple times. If he could do what he did, then how can we really know anyone is safe?

> (**BRITTANY** *enters as if she's cutting through to somewhere else – class?*)

Hey Brittany!

BRITTANY. Hey!

MICHELLE. We heard you're going to prom with Dylan.

BRITTANY. Yeah. He jumped out of a cake.

MICHELLE. *(Unsure.)* That's sweet...

KAYLA. He asked you in front of everyone in the cafeteria!

BRITTANY. I thought he was talking to Megan. I didn't even realize he was talking to *me* until everyone was looking at me.

MICHELLE. Weird.

BRITTANY. Yeah, and then I just heard myself saying yes, and it was over...

Anyway, see you guys in class.

> (**BRITTANY** *leaves.*)

KAYLA. Yuck.

MICHELLE. No, no, don't give me that look. We can do this. We have the highest combined GPA in the whole school, we can figure out how to get the right guys to ask us to prom.

KAYLA. This might be more difficult than Ms. William's AP Lang class.

> *(Lights switch to the other side of the cafetorium.* **TERRY**, **ALEX**, *and* **JIMMY** *enter and sit at a cafeteria table.)*

TERRY. They just don't make sense.

ALEX. Right?!

TERRY. It's like, don't look at me, look at me, but don't look at me like that, but think I'm hot, but then don't touch me or say anything. Like what am I supposed to do?

ALEX. Right?!

TERRY. Jimmy, don't you have sisters?

JIMMY. Yeah, but they're little. Eight and ten.

ALEX. You have a *mom*.

TERRY. Moms are different.

ALEX. But they were girls once.

TERRY. I guess.

JIMMY. I don't want to think about my mom being hot.

ALEX. Your mom is hot.

JIMMY. Dude, back off my mom.

ALEX. Sorry, bro, facts.

TERRY. He's right.

JIMMY. Whatever, she's not a girl. She's a mom, MY mom.

TERRY. Fair, fair.

What I want to know about is regular girls.

The Annas, Maddies, and Evas.

What makes them tick?

ALEX. They want to be hot.

> And then the want to control us with their hotness.

> They're basically aliens out to control us through our raging hormones, so we'll like buy them stuff.

TERRY. You're basically saying they're the government.

JIMMY. My sisters are just kids, they play softball and try to beat me at video games.

TERRY. Girls play video games?

ALEX. Before they get boobs and become mind control robots.

JIMMY. You guys are so stupid.

ALEX. Hey!

JIMMY. We've been going to school with girls our whole lives. They're just girls.

ALEX. Then you explain all this shit they expect us to do? Text them, tell them they're hot, but don't ask for pics, but put on the moves, but not if they say no, but Ethan said she didn't say anything, so what are we supposed to do?

TERRY. Right?!

JIMMY. Dude, shut up! You don't know anything about girls.

ALEX. I KNOW! Were you even listening?

JIMMY. Why don't you idiots ask a GIRL?!

TERRY. Bro, social suicide.

ALEX. And they're not going to tell us anyway.

> Ethan said –

JIMMY. Ethan is a douchebag, OK.

> You shouldn't listen to anything he says.

ALEX. He's our friend.

JIMMY. He assaulted that girl.

ALEX. He says it wasn't –

JIMMY. And you believe him?

TERRY. It's his word against hers.

ALEX. They were drinking –

TERRY. Exactly, like if you're both drunk –

JIMMY. OK, Terry, how many shots until you don't care what I do to you?

ALEX. Whoa, dude.

JIMMY. What? Isn't that what you're saying?

If you're drunk, if she's drunk, you can just do what you want.

ALEX. Jimmy, calm down.

JIMMY. No.

Girls, they're people.

They're not robots or spies or aliens.

They're just people.

ALEX. Yeah, we're just goofing around.

JIMMY. I don't think you are.

(**JIMMY** *storms out.*)

TERRY. Dude, I didn't know Jimmy's gay.

ALEX. Oh, for god's sake, Terry!

(Promposal transition: Promposal of your choice, should emphasize that the identity of the girl saying yes doesn't really matter.)

(From the original production: Two **GIRLS** *from the ensemble walk across stage chatting.*

A **BOY** *comes up behind them holding a promposal sign.*

BOY. Hey, one of yous...

The **GIRLS** *wrestle between themselves to push the other toward the* **BOY**. *They land side by side.*

BOY. Prom?

The **GIRLS** *look at each other and shrug in resigned agreement. They turn to leave.*

BOY. Yes! Two!

He exits after them.)

Scene 5: Prom-Dump-als

(**STEPH**, **REINA**, *and* **TRENT** *walk across the stage on the way to class. Projection: "30 Days Until Prom."* **STEPH** *shows her phone to* **TRENT**.)

STEPH. Did you see that Ethan's back in town?

REINA. How do you know that?

TRENT. His mom posted a picture of them at Bob Evans.

REINA. Weird.

STEPH. He can't come to school, right?

REINA. Why would he?

STEPH. Other people do, visiting from college.

TRENT. Is your mom going to do anything? About all the news?

STEPH. *The Golden Apple* article's been reposted all over.

REINA. I'm glad my mom only really uses WhatsApp or she'd be totally freaked.

They're going to do all the usual things, a committee...

She said something about an anti-harassment policy as part of the new code of conduct, but some parents are upset about using the word "sex."

TRENT. As if seeing the word would make us all lose our minds.

REINA. sex, sex, sex, sex, sex, SEX!

TRENT. The urges, the urges are taking me over!

STEPH. Oh! No, stop! I can't take it!

REINA. That's exactly what they think, that we can't control ourselves.

TRENT. That boys can't.

REINA. Of course they can. They just don't because people don't expect them to.

TRENT. I mean, sure they might get a *(Mimes an erection.)* without meaning to, but it's not like you have to *do* anything with it. If you just leave it alone, it'll go away.

STEPH. I went to that anti-sexual-assault teach-in at the clinic.

REINA. I meant to go. How was it?

STEPH. Kind of depressing. There were lots of statistics about how sexual assault and domestic abuse cases don't get convicted and how dangerous it is to try and leave an abusive relationship.

It's like these guys hear "no" and totally flip out. It's scary.

> *(**REINA** has a realization.)*

REINA. You ever notice that girls never say no to the promposals?

STEPH. Somebody must…

> *(She looks to **TRENT**.)*

TRENT. I can't think of anyone.

REINA. And we know those girls don't always want to go – Brittany definitely doesn't want to go with *Dylan Morris*!

TRENT. No one does.

STEPH. But if she said no, he'd be embarrassed. And people would say she's mean. Or worse –

TRENT. Slut, whore, skank –

STEPH. Or the opposite: prude, frigid, ice queen.

REINA. Exactly! And this isn't any date, this is PROM

– with maybe kissing or hooking up – because it's prom.

REINA. They're on dates with these guys they don't even really like 'cause they couldn't say no in front of all those people, how are they gonna say no to anything when they're alone together?

TRENT. That is so dark.

STEPH. Eww, eww, eww! No one should go to prom or on dates until we're all old, like thirty-five!

REINA. No, we need to teach the girls to say NO and people – boys – how to be rejected, without turning into violent doxing incels.

TRENT. What about those of us who don't fit in tidy pink or blue boxes?

REINA. Same principle applies – ask and answer without fear!

TRENT. Fair, we have enough issues with normies. We don't want to take on their bad relationship habits.

REINA. We need guys to see other guys getting rejected and not freaking out so that girls can say no, if they want to. "Prom-dump-als."

TRENT. It doesn't have the same ring.

REINA. Work in progress.

STEPH. We need a dude.

TRENT. Adam?

STEPH. Ehh.

(She shrugs.)

TRENT. *(To* **STEPH**.*)* He's your friend.

STEPH. Is he? He's just kind of around.

REINA. OK, but he likes you best. Will you text him?

Say it's like a prank or method acting or something.

STEPH. I'll ask, but if he says no, *you* have to be really chill about it.

*(She texts **ADAM**.)*

TRENT. We're going to need to make his promposal really good, otherwise people will know it's a setup.

REINA. Good point. We should start researching prompo–

STEPH. He's in.

REINA. Really?

STEPH. *(Reading.)* "Yea, sure. I'm in.

I got accepted to U of C and I don't want ppl thinking I'm a creep

Don't tell Reina and Trent LOL

I don't want to look like a simp."

Oops.

REINA. Steph you're going to have to keep this a secret. If people find out we planned this, it's not going to be pretty.

STEPH. Right, yes. I can do that.

Scene 6: Just Ask

(A portion of the cafetorium is transformed into a small office. Projections show a U of C slide. **ETHAN** *paces while* **DR. GRAY** *sits.)*

ETHAN. I shouldn't have to apologize!

If I have to apologize then she should too.

She led me on.

DR. GRAY. Why do you think that?

ETHAN. She'd flirt with me after class, sit near me and giggle and whatever.

We were at the Delta Beta party, it was chill, I could tell she was into me.

I asked if I could walk her home, I was trying to be a good guy.

DR. GRAY. It sounds like she liked you.

ETHAN. See!

DR. GRAY. But that doesn't mean she was ready to be sexual with you.

ETHAN. It was just kissing.

DR. GRAY. Kissing can be a big deal to people.

Did you ask Lindsey if she wanted to kiss you?

ETHAN. You don't do that. You don't *talk*.

You just like, lean in.

DR. GRAY. Then how do you know what your partner wants?

ETHAN. Girls like, make noises and push on you.

DR. GRAY. How do you know what the noises mean?

ETHAN. I dunno.

DR. GRAY. Do you think it's possible that the noises you thought meant yes, Lindsey thinks meant no?

ETHAN. Maybe.

DR. GRAY. Maybe?

How could you know for sure?

ETHAN. I dunno! Ask her!

DR. GRAY. Exactly.

Ask. Her.

ETHAN. You don't ask, nobody *asks*!

DR. GRAY. Actually, lots of people do.

ETHAN. And what if she says no? Are you a pervert loser then too?

DR. GRAY. Not if you stop.

ETHAN. *(Mocking.)* "Do you want to have sexual relations with me?"

That's so embarrassing.

DR. GRAY. There are worse things than feeling embarrassed.

Do you think you would be in this situation if you'd asked Lindsey what she wanted?

ETHAN. No.

DR. GRAY. OK, that's a start.

Scene 7: No-ball

(The cafetorium. The whole **ENSEMBLE** *is onstage.* **BRITTANY** *sits near a group of* **GIRLS***, and* **DYLAN** *sits with a group of* **BOYS***. The projections promote prom: "Dukes and Princesses, oh my!"* **ADAM** *is at the end of a grand romantic gesture [think boom box over head, end of a love song, or holding up a giant heart-shaped poster board with "go to prom with me?" on it] directed to* **STEPH***, standing next to him.* **REINA** *and* **TRENT** *record on their phones from different areas of the stage.)*

ADAM. Steph! It's all about you, girl, will you be my prom date?

STEPH. Adam, wow, that's really nice. And you're really great, I mean you're a good person, you're fun, and this was really unexpected and, uh, I – um, No. No, I won't go to prom with you.

ENSEMBLE. Ooooooh, damn!

What? what!

She did not!

What a –!

(This gets cut off by **ADAM***.)*

ADAM. Oh, OK. That's cool.

ENSEMBLE. Excuse me?

He said what?

STEPH. Yeah?

ADAM. I mean, it's kind of a bummer. But, ah, no hard feelings. I only want you to go with me if that's what you really want to do. And if it's not, that's OK. We're cool.

ENSEMBLE. Huh?

Yeah, I mean, I guess that's alright, or whatever.

Damn, he grown.

STEPH. Um, great, uh, so...lunch?

ADAM. Yeah, I'm just gonna, you know, put this stuff away.

> (**ADAM** *exits.* **STEPH** *goes to join* **REINA** *and* **TRENT** *at their lunch table.* **BRITTANY** *begins to realize she can make a new choice.*)

STEPH. Ohmygod, ohmygod, ohmygod. I can't – I can't – believe –

I just did that, in front of everyone.

EVERYONE!

REINA. You were awesome!

TRENT. Yes, great rejection!

STEPH. I know it wasn't real, but it felt so real!

Everybody watching, wanting you to say yes.

It was like I could hear them in my head chanting.

It's so much pressure! I mean, I knew, but didn't know!

Ohmygod.

What did I say? I can't remember.

TRENT. Do you want to watch it?

STEPH. No!

TRENT. Look at you! Just rolls off the tongue!

REINA. You did all the things we practiced, you were really complimentary, and then you just said no, you didn't give any reasons.

STEPH. Is that OK?

REINA. Of course!

> (**ADAM** *joins their table.*)

ADAM. Wooo! That was awesome! Up top, Steph.

> *(He tries to give* **STEPH** *a high five.* **REINA** *or* **TRENT** *pulls his hand down.)*

REINA. Shhhh! Be chill!

ADAM. But, come on, admit it. I was all sincere and understanding and cool, like actually cool.

REINA. I guess.

ADAM. Have you ever seen anyone keep their shit together like that?

TRENT. Yes.

REINA. You hold yourself to a very low bar.

ADAM. Whatever, my DMs are fire! That clip is already all over, and girls are totally into it! I might actually get a *real* prom date.

> *(***BRITTANY*** approaches ***DYLAN***.)*

REINA. This isn't about that.

ADAM. Eh, but it doesn't hurt.

TRENT. Shh, shh! Y'all, check it out.

BRITTANY. Um, Dylan, I know what I said, and what you did was really impressive, the cake thing – but, no. I'm not going to prom with you.

ENSEMBLE. You go, girl!

Speak your truth, honey!

DYLAN. What the he–

ENSEMBLE. Whoa, dude, be cool.

She's just being real with you.

It's not a big deal.

DYLAN. Uh, I mean, whatever. I don't get it, but that's your choice.

(**DYLAN** *exits; the rest of the* **ENSEMBLE** *at the boys' table follows him.*)

ENSEMBLE. Right on, man.

Good on you, Dylan.

(**BRITTANY** *comes over to* **STEPH**.)

BRITTANY. You are my hero! My shero!

I didn't want to go with him, but I just didn't even think I could say no, which feels silly now, but anyway, thanks girl.

(**BRITTANY** *and the rest of the* **GIRL ENSEMBLE** *exit.* **ADAM** *follows them, hoping for a date.* **STEPH** *turns to* **REINA** *in delight.*)

STEPH. OMG! Brittany!!!

REINA. I think this just might work!

(**EM** *walks up to their table.*)

Wh– uh, hi, Em.

EM. Did you all plan that?

STEPH. What? No!

EM. OK, well it was cool.

REINA. Really?

EM. Yeah, more people here should really know about consent.

REINA. Definitely!

EM. And you can't really give it, consent, under pressure.

REINA. Right! Exactly.

TRENT. Did you learn that in your peer educator training?

EM. Yes, actually. We cover all aspects of sex ed not just STIs and abstinence like at school.

TRENT. Riiight.

EM. Our next workshop is on healthy queer relationships, how things can look different for us because of stigma and gender identity, you might want to check it out.

TRENT. *(Begrudgingly.)* That does sound interesting.

EM. Yeah, anyway. See you in math, Reina.

REINA. Cool, yeah. Math.

EM. Later.

> *(They leave.)*

STEPH. I thought we couldn't tell anyone?

REINA. I didn't, not really.

STEPH. Except you basically did.

REINA. Em's down.

STEPH. Or you just want to be down with Em…

REINA. What, no! Whatever!   **TRENT.** Veto!

What's your deal with them anyway?

TRENT. Where do I even begin? They're so –

STEPH. You guuuysss, listen!

> *(A crescendo of "Nos" from backstage; maybe a balloon is released so that it flies haphazardly and runs out of air; distorted pop music.*)*

---

* A license to produce THIS IS NOT A TEEN MOVIE does not include a performance license for any third-party or copyrighted music. Licensees should create an original composition or use music in the public domain. For further information, please see the Music and Third-Party Materials Use Note on page iii.

Scene 8: Two Sides of the Same Coin

(A few days later. Projection: "14 Days Until Prom." **DYLAN, JIMMY,** *and* **ALEX** *are walking through the cafetorium.* **TERRY** *enters with some promposal accessories that are either generic or look beat-up.)*

TERRY. Another one bites the dust.

ALEX. What's your count bro?

TERRY. I'm up to twelve – but Brittany was kinda mean about it.

JIMMY. That's because everyone and their brother is asking her – she basically has to shout NO at every dude that even looks at her.

DYLAN. Whatever, I was the first.

JIMMY. Are you bragging about that?

DYLAN. Shut up, Jimmy. What's your count, oh yeah, ZERO! Cause you're too chickenshit to ask anyone.

ALEX. Yeah, why don't you just take your little sister?

JIMMY. Why do I hang out with you guys?

*(***JIMMY*** leaves. ***ALEX*** calls after him.)*

ALEX. Come on, man, don't take everything so seriously! We're just joking.

TERRY. Bro, hear me out, what if Jimmy really is gay?

ALEX. OK, so what? That's fine.

DYLAN. What if he's into you?! Dude gross!

TERRY. Nah, Jimmy's not into me.

ALEX. I've known Jimmy my whole life, and even if he did want this hot male specimen in front of you, who could blame him? Jimmy's cool, he wouldn't be a creep about it – unlike some people I know.

DYLAN. Who are you calling a creep?

ALEX. I didn't name any names. You just assumed.

DYLAN. Screw you, Alex! I didn't know you were all a bunch of sissies now.

> (**DYLAN** *leaves.*)

TERRY. Dude, do you think Dylan is gay?

ALEX. Terry, that is not the answer to everything!

TERRY. Come on? Be real.

ALEX. Fine.

Maybe?

Maybe e*veryone* is kinda gay.

TERRY. *Bro! EVERYONE?!*

> (**BRITTANY** *walks on, cutting through to class; when she sees them, she points and shouts.*)

BRITTANY. NO. NO.

ALEX. Yeah, OK, no one's asking.

> (**TERRY** *and* **ALEX** *exit.* **MICHELLE** *and* **KAYLA** *are sitting on the edge of the stage.*)

KAYLA. Wow, do you shout like that at everyone now?

BRITTANY. NO.

I mean, yeah.

MICHELLE. How many times have you been asked to prom?

BRITTANY. I lost count.

I don't even wait for them to ask, I just shout NO.

KAYLA. That's kinda cool.

I don't think I could handle all the attention.

MICHELLE. But don't you want a prom date?

I mean, you're so pretty.

KAYLA. *(Giving* **MICHELLE** *a look.)* And *smart*.

MICHELLE. What? They're not mutually exclusive.

BRITTANY. Thanks, but I'm not smart like you two, I have to study *a lot*.

MICHELLE. We study all the time! That's why we don't have friends.

KAYLA. I don't want a lot of friends.

Just good friends, *(To* **MICHELLE**.*)* like you.

MICHELLE. Aww, thanks girl.

BRITTANY. I wish I had a friend like that.

MICHELLE. But you're so popular!

You're always going to parties and stuff.

We've seen your Stories.

Not that we're stalking you or anything.

BRITTANY. That's just *(Air quotes.)* "pretty girl" stuff.

KAYLA. Huh?

MICHELLE. I mean you are very pretty –

KAYLA. Very pretty...

MICHELLE. But...?

BRITTANY. It's so embarrassing.

MICHELLE. Spill!

BRITTANY. OK, so my family moves around a lot for my mom's job, she does some sort of high-level consulting work that requires her to "be a presence," which means no remote.

BRITTANY. Anyway, moving a bunch in middle school was the worst, but in seventh grade, I figured out there's always room for another "pretty girl" – not the prettiest girl in the center of the picture, but another one in the group, – at the cafeteria table, at the party. Not a real friend, but somebody extra who gets invited to stuff and that was better than being alone.

MICHELLE. That sounds kinda sad.

KAYLA. But it also kinda solved your problem, so good for you?

BRITTANY. Do you want to hear my "pretty girl" rules?

MICHELLE. Yeah!

BRITTANY. 1. Be nice to *everyone*.

MICHELLE.	**KAYLA.**
So difficult.	Exhausting.

BRITTANY. 2. Look cute, but not too cute – you know what I mean.

MICHELLE.	**KAYLA.**
Look good, but don't get dress-coded.	Nice, but don't stand out.

BRITTANY. 3. Only post the right pictures. And then try to figure out the right captions!

MICHELLE.	**KAYLA.**
The balance is so difficult!	I don't post, too much pressure.

BRITTANY. 4. Never have too strong of an opinion except about girly things like Olivia Rodrigo and Sabrina Carpenter.

MICHELLE.	**KAYLA.**
Sabrina!	Olivia!

BRITTANY. 5. "Take a joke" even when it's definitely not a joke.

KAYLA. It's never a joke.

MICHELLE. Ever.

BRITTANY. I've never told anybody about that before.

MICHELLE. You should write an article for *The Golden Apple*, "Confessions of a 'Pretty Girl.'"

BRITTANY. Really?

KAYLA. I don't mean to be rude, but I think those are just girl rules.

You're just also really pretty, so they made you popular.

But, we basically do that stuff too.

MICHELLE. And we're not popular.

BRITTANY. So? You have real friends.
The people I hang out with don't talk about anything real.
It's like they're all bots.
And when Dylan asked me to prom, they were so weird about it, like he's a catch just because he's a jock.

And, he says things sometimes, not to me, but to other guys...
And I kept wondering what if Dylan's like *Ethan* –
And what I would do if he tried something?

And I was scared I wouldn't do anything.
So when I saw a chance to change my mind, I said no.

KAYLA. That must have been really hard for you.

BRITTANY. I guess.

Yeah.

Ohmygod. I've been talking so much.

KAYLA. It's totally OK.

BRITTANY. Are you all going to prom?

Do you have dates?

MICHELLE. My mom is being super weird about the whole no-date thing.

I've tried to explain to her that literally NOBODY has a date anymore, but she thinks I'm lying.

BRITTANY. Right! My mom keeps being like, but what about the pictures?

KAYLA. My mom is definitely more excited about prom than I am. It's like she wants to fix her high school mistakes through me.

BRITTANY. I just want to get dressed up and dance and have fun.

MICHELLE. I want to be a pretty, pretty princess for one night!

KAYLA. I want to dance to the three songs I know, eat cake, and spend the rest of the night on the patio looking at everyone's outfits.

MICHELLE. *(Squeezing* **KAYLA.***)* Yes! Progress!

KAYLA. What if we all went to prom together?

BRITTANY. Me too? Really?

MICHELLE. Yeah, you're our friend now.

KAYLA. Now that we've talked about some real stuff.

BRITTANY. Aww, you guys!

(They exit making plans.)

(Rejection transition: A rejection/reversal of the first promposal transition.)

(From the original production: **BOY** *with police hat is walking across the stage.* **GIRL** *enters.*

GIRL. Stop! Freeze!

BOY *stops. She walks up to him and takes his hat and puts it on.*

GIRL. No. I won't go to prom with you. Who even asks somebody like that!

She walks off. **BOY** *follows and shows his rejection count going up on a poster board.)*

Scene 9: Not What I Expected

(Cafetorium. Projection: "Please Buy Prom Tickets! We have to get decorations." **REINA** *is writing in her journal/talking to the audience.)*

REINA. Dear Diary, things are going well?!
Sort of?
People aren't accepting promposals they don't want which is great.
But it seems like no one has a date to prom.
Which I guess is fine?
though that wasn't really the point.

Luckily, no one's figured out we staged Adam and Steph's promposal.
Plus one for stealth!

But, boys are competing to see who can get rejected the most times.
Which should be fun but isn't.
There are more promposals than ever – which is awful.
So maybe things aren't going that well?

Steph and Trent are planning our prom outfits –
which are a little too theme adjacent for me,
but they're so excited about them and I don't *really* care...
OK, except – OK – I do really care.
Because it's not a costume party!
And I still want a real date.
Which seems even more ridiculous now –

EM. Hey, uh. Reina?

*(***REINA*** *quickly closes her notebook.)*

REINA. Em, hey!

You look great, I mean, I don't mean to just comment on how you look...

EM. It's cool. Thanks.

REINA. Yeah.

EM. What are you writing?

REINA. Oh, it's just my homework.

Uh, not homework-homework

Therapy homework.

EM. Cool.

REINA. Yeah, I have a lot of...feelings.

EM. That's good.

REINA. I guess.

(*Awkward but cute pause.*)

EM. Steph's been coming to a lot of workshops down at the clinic.

REINA. Yeah, uh,

EM. How come you don't come too?

REINA. I, uh, no real reason.

EM. It's not 'cause your mom is the principal, is it?

REINA. No! No, my mom is very supportive of all forms of education, it's just –

...

I find like the whole thing kind of intimidating.

EM. Do you think I'm intimidating?

REINA. Kind of...

But in a good way.

You just seem so sure of yourself.

EM. I guess I am sure of some things.

But I'm trying to figure out a lot of stuff too.

REINA. Like what?

EM. Feelings.

REINA. Yeah, haha, me too!

> (**TRENT** *enters unseen by* **EM** *and* **REINA**; *they eavesdrop.*)

EM. Reina, will you go to prom with me?

REINA. Oh, uh, what?

EM. Will you go to prom with me, as my date?

REINA. I, uh, I wasn't expecting you to say that.

EM. OK?

> *(They both sit awkwardly for a moment.)*

Did I mess up? I just didn't think you'd be into the big promposal thing, Steph said you were pretty anti–

REINA. You asked Steph about me?

EM. Yeah. I mean we were talking at the consent workshop about the stuff you all are doing –

> (**TRENT** *walks up like they've just arrived.*)

TRENT. Hey Reina! You ready? Your mom's looking for you.

REINA. Hey, yeah. Just let me get my stuff.

TRENT. Em, hey. What are you doing here?

EM. Just talking.

(To **REINA**.*)* Let me know what you decide.

See you later.

> (**EM** *leaves.*)

REINA. Why are you always so rude to Em?

TRENT. I'm not.

REINA. You are.

TRENT. What does it matter? I just don't like them.

Come on, they're just so…self-righteous.

REINA. So are we.

TRENT. Yes, but we're right and fun and attractive.

REINA. They're attractive.

TRENT. Uggghhh, can we not talk about Em? We've got to go, I want to stay on your mom's good side.

REINA. My mom loves you.

TRENT. At least someone's mom does!

REINA. Is your mom being all weird again?

TRENT. Always, but thankfully she's on one of her retreats this weekend.

Can I sleep over? And Steph too? We can practice our prom makeup!

REINA. Yeah, sure.

(**REINA** *looks in the direction* **EM** *exited. Then she and* **TRENT** *leave the other way.*)

Scene 10: Social Media

(A portion of the cafetorium is transformed into a small office. The projection has a U of C slide.)

DR. GRAY. Why did you delete your social media?

ETHAN. My lawyer –

DR. GRAY. Before that…

ETHAN. Those people don't know me!

DR. GRAY. Some of them do.

ETHAN. Not the REAL me, and they were saying stuff, like that I was a monster and what they were going to do to me if I came around their girlfriends or daughters or whatever, old guys tryin' to act tough.

DR. GRAY. Did any of the threats cause you concern?

ETHAN. Some of them knew my address – my parents' address!

DR. GRAY. But they're just words?

ETHAN. You're not supposed to say stuff like that.

DR. GRAY. Like what?

ETHAN. You're trying to make me feel stupid.

DR. GRAY. I'm trying to help you draw a parallel between how you felt when people made threatening comments to you and your own online comments toward Lindsey.

ETHAN. She pissed me off.

DR. GRAY. Because she reported you.

ETHAN. That stuff is supposed to be private.

DR. GRAY. Dates? Sexual activities? Or reports of assault?

You've never told anyone about your experiences with other partners?

ETHAN. That's different, locker-room stuff, not like her telling everyone on campus I'm a pervert. It was just kissing.

DR. GRAY. Kissing someone without consent is sexual assault.

ETHAN. I would have stopped if she'd asked.

DR. GRAY. We've been over this. You wouldn't have to stop if you'd asked in the first place.

ETHAN. Why did she have to tell everybody about it?

DR. GRAY. She didn't, you did. She only told campus administration.

ETHAN. Well someone in "campus administration" told everybody 'cause the next morning my RA told me I had a disciplinary meeting and then everyone in my dorm was saying I was a predator.

I'm not! I haven't even done that, I haven't gone all the way. I'm just a freshman.

DR. GRAY. You called Lindsey a liar, you degraded her appearance and character. You went into great detail about where and how you would attack her. You posted links to her social media and asked others to join you in harassing her.

ETHAN. I was mad.

DR. GRAY. Well, what did it do?! Did it make you feel better? Because it certainly turned your moment of failed courtship, which could probably have been resolved with mediation by the way, into a full-scale all-campus Title IX "Incident."

ETHAN. I'm not gonna lie, it felt good at first.

The other guys, they understood me, how I was feeling,

But some of the stuff got out of hand, Lindsey blocked me and then my dad called me, he was so angry, scary angry. My little sister had seen what I posted.

ETHAN. And then I got kicked off campus, and I might lose my spot on the team, my scholarship

My sister, she'll talk to me, but it's different, like she's nervous

My parents – they don't know what to do.

DR. GRAY. You were ashamed and embarrassed and you lashed out.

ETHAN. I made a mistake.

DR. GRAY. Yes, you did.

ETHAN. Now what?

DR. GRAY. As I see it, you have two choices.

You can continue to double down on this mistake, like you did when you attacked Lindsey online.

Or you can take responsibility for your actions, show her and all those people that you understand what you did was wrong.

ETHAN. Nobody does that.

DR. GRAY. You've started trends before.

(Rejection transition: A rejection where a group of **BOYS** *tries to rack up rejections and the* **GIRLS** *turn on them.)*

(From the original production: A group of three **GIRLS** *walk together across the stage. A pair of* **BOYS** *comes up behind them. The* **BOYS** *ask each* **GIRL** *to prom; all say no. The* **BOYS** *record their tally on small whiteboards. The* **GIRLS** *circle the* **BOYS** *saying NO repeatedly and chase them offstage.)*

Scene 11: Investigative Reporting

(The cafetorium. **KRIS** *interviews* **STEPH** *and* **ADAM**.*)*

KRIS. As the first public failed promposal, are there any hard feelings between you two?

STEPH. No?

KRIS. Is that a question?

STEPH. No. No!

KRIS. Adam?

ADAM. No, it's cool. We're cool.

STEPH. Yeah, there's no story here. We're just friends, and it was sooo weird and unexpected and totally not planned at all and I just wouldn't *ever* consider Adam for any kind of date, like not even to Target – so definitely not PROM! I mean, oh my god – gosh – goodgollymissmolly – whew –

ADAM. We've been to Target.

STEPH. Not on a date!

ADAM. Who goes on a date to Target?

KRIS. Oookay.

After your "encounter" here in the cafeteria, there's been a trend to reject promposals. What do you think of that?

*(***STEPH*** shakes her head; she can't talk.)*

ADAM. That...we're...influencers!

Do you think I could get sponsored?

I'm planning on pursuing acting and I know casting directors take you more seriously if you have a lot of followers.

STEPH. What brand wants to be identified with rejection?

ADAM. Not, rejection, but keeping cool in the face of rejection.

Like deodorant? Or Red Bull? Prime? They sponsored archery...

STEPH. What?!

KRIS. Adam, you're an actor?

ADAM. A thespian!

Don't you remember, I was the understudy for Danny in *Grease*?

KRIS. Right...and you're friends.

> *(They all look at each other.* **KRIS** *is putting the pieces together.)*

STEPH. Pleeease don't tell anyone we planned it!

ADAM. It was a class project.

STEPH. It was?

ADAM. AP Psych and Guerilla Theatre.

Yeah, Augusto Boal!

STEPH. Reina thought if people saw a guy getting rejected and NOT melting down like a big baby then people could say no, if they wanted to.

KRIS. Reina?

Principal Baldwin's daughter?

This was her idea?

STEPH. No!   **ADAM**. Yeah.

ADAM. OK, Reina came up with it, but we should definitely get credit because we're the ones that went through with it.

KRIS. Was Principal Baldwin involved?

STEPH & ADAM. No!

KRIS. Sure.

STEPH. Come on, Kris! You have to see that it's objectively better for people to get to say no.

KRIS. I'm a journalist. I'm impartial.

What I know now is that you conspired with the principal's daughter to undermine a school tradition and the people deserve to know.

*(**KRIS** starts to pack up to leave.)*

STEPH. Tradition?

KRIS. Based on our social media numbers and *Golden Apple* web traffic, Golden Valley High is known for sports and promposals, and your actions have reduced us to just sports.

ADAM. What about the plays?

The glee club?

Band won state!

STEPH. Wait, Kris isn't the real story here that it's time for new traditions?

And supporting the arts?

ADAM. Yeah, this was political street theatre!

KRIS. *(Exiting.)* I'll consider that angle.

But I'm publishing in the next issue, so be prepared.

The DEAR GVH Facebook group is going to try and figure out what rules you broke and come for you.

*(**ADAM** and **STEPH** look at each other and run offstage in the other direction.)*

Scene 12: Cult of Prom

*(A small thrift store – a rack of clothes and a "Spiffy Thrift" projection. **REINA** and **JACYLN** shop for prom dresses; after all, **JACYLN** has to go to prom too. Throughout this dialogue, they show each other options and can ad-lib responses [yes, no, too flashy, etc.].)*

REINA. I'm not in a cult.

JACYLN. Oh-ho-no! You are apparently the founder of a lesbian separatist feminist cult.

REINA. They don't know what feminist separatists are.

JACYLN. True. What they said was a lot meaner, but that's what it boils down to.

REINA. And people are just queer now.

JACYLN. Some people fought really hard for those labels you want to throw out, but that's not what we need to talk about right now. You've stirred up the "not all men" crew, and they're trying to figure out what rules you've broken –

REINA. I haven't broken any rules –

JACYLN. Or if you're acting as my agent –

REINA. Hahaha! Seriously?

JACYLN. Yes! These people need to get a grip. If I knew how to get you to do my bidding, I'd make better use of it than ruining prom.

REINA. MOM! I'm not ruining prom.

JACYLN. I know, I know. Now, tell me the truth. Is this about those college kids?

REINA. Maybe.

JACYLN. Honey, you need to let the adults handle it.

REINA. With what? A newsletter? This is a big deal, something needed to be done.

JACYLN. There are official channels. It takes systemic changes to take on systemic problems.

REINA. But all that just takes sooo long.

JACYLN. I know it feels that way, but real, substantial changes take time –

REINA. You don't understand. This is my only senior prom, I have to do it now. I don't just want it to be better for other people later, I want it to be better for me now.

JACYLN. Reina, I want that for you too. You just take on so much. I want you to enjoy this time.

REINA. Oh, I loved watching Steph shut Adam down, even if it was fake.

And I might, sort of, maybe have a prom date.

JACYLN. Whooo?

REINA. Em.

JACYLN. *Em.* OK, you two certainly have shared interests.

REINA. Right!

It's just...

I was kinda disappointed when they asked.

I thought – it would feel bigger, more exciting.

JACYLN. You wanted fireworks and butterflies and all that love story stuff.

REINA. yeah.

JACYLN. It's mostly not like that.

REINA. I know.

I just didn't know what to do, and then Trent showed up and I haven't given Em an answer and I don't know if I've waited too long.

And I keep thinking about Trent and Steph and all the prom stuff –

REINA. How do you know how to make the right decision?

JACYLN. *(Grabbing a dress.)* Sometimes you just know and sometimes you have to try things out and see what happens.

This one?

REINA. I'll try it on!

> (**REINA** *takes the dress and goes to try it on.* **JACYLN** *keeps looking through the racks.* **TRENT** *and* **STEPH** *enter.)*

TRENT. Look for really big headbands or old Sunday hats – we can use them as the base for the headpieces.

STEPH. Reminding you to steer closer to Met Gala than Coachella here.

TRENT. Why can't we have the best of both worlds?

It's Jacyln! I mean, hey, Principal Baldwin. What're you up to?

JACYLN. Prom shopping. I'm head chaperone now! I've got to find something that is cute and comfortable.

TRENT. Please, please, please let me style you! Steph and Reina and I are all going together as The Gender Inclusive Sisterhood of the Traveling Queens highly influenced by *Drag Race* Season 8.

JACYLN. You got that from "Hollywood Royalty"?

TRENT. Uh-huh! We're just here looking for bases for the headpieces.

JACYLN. That's a choice.

STEPH. Yeah, we're just popping in, Trent's going to give me a ride to the clinic.

TRENT. I am?

STEPH. Yeah, there's a workshop on setting healthy boundaries that I want to go to.

JACYLN. Isn't Em a peer educator at the clinic?

TRENT. *(Annoyed.)* Yes.

*(Seeing **STEPH**'s annoyance at their comment.)* But, it's so great you're going Steph – balance out the vibes.

STEPH. *(To **TRENT**.)* Right.

*(To **JACYLN**.)* I'm thinking of doing something health or education related in college. I don't know yet.

JACYLN. I can't believe you all will be headed off to college so soon! It feels like just last week you all were having a *Hannah Montana* sing-along in the basement.

STEPH. That was last week!   **TRENT.** Don't out us like that!

JACYLN. I'm just teasing. Though, Trent, I have noticed you've been spending a lot of time at the house. Is everything OK at home?

STEPH. I'm just going to look over at hats.

*(As she steps away from the conversation/exits to get hats, to **TRENT**.)* Remember we've got to go soon.

TRENT. *(To **STEPH**.)* Oookay.

*(To **JACYLN**.)* It's not like anything you need to report – it's just –

They don't get me – and I can't explain *me* to them without them trying to tell me I'm wrong about who I am, so now we just don't talk at all. It's *very* awkward. So, I'd just rather not be there.

JACYLN. That has to be really hard on you. You always have a spot at our house, even if Reina isn't home, OK?

TRENT. Thanks Jacyln.

*(They hug. **REINA** comes out in a prom dress.)*

REINA. Hey Mom, look!

JACYLN. Oh! It's beautiful!

REINA. Trent, hey.

TRENT. Is that a prom dress?

REINA. I'm just looking.

TRENT. Why?

REINA. ...

TRENT. WHY!

JACYLN. Trent, honey, take a breath.

>(**STEPH** *runs over with an armful of hats.*)

TRENT. I've been working for *weeks* on our prom ensembles, for the *THREE* of us. And while Steph and I are picking up the final touches –

STEPH. Headpieces! Met Gala!

REINA. They only wear them on the red carpet!

STEPH. Prom is the red carpet of high school!

TRENT. You're here – what? Shopping for some generic dress so you can look like a knockoff princess like every other girl at prom?

REINA. Maybe I want my own look instead of being one of your accessories.

TRENT. Then you should have said so weeks ago before I made you a dress!

STEPH. It's mostly alterations.

TRENT. Steph!

JACYLN. I think we all need to take a break –

TRENT. You're right! I'm out of here.

>(**TRENT** *storms out.*)

STEPH. Sorry, Trent's my ride.

I'll try and...you know.

(**STEPH** *runs after* **TRENT**, *unintentionally stealing the hats she's holding.*)

JACYLN. It's OK, baby. You all can work it out.

REINA. It's not fair!

We always do what Trent wants.

JACYLN. Trent does have strong opinions,

But honey, so do you.

And it sounds like you haven't been totally honest with them.

REINA. Because I knew this would happen.

JACYLN. OK, we'll talk about that later.

(**JACYLN** *hugs* **REINA**.)

Do you want to get this dress?

REINA. Is it OK, even if I change my mind later?

JACYLN. Yes, you don't always know exactly what you want in the moment.

Come on, let's get going. Do you want to stop for boba on the way home?

REINA. Yes.

(*Rejection transition: A full ensemble number! Emphasizing that the rejections are taking over.*)

(*From the original production: A* West Side Story/*"Beat It" style dance-off where the* **GIRL ENSEMBLE** *enters, snapping their fingers and chanting "no," while the* **BOY ENSEMBLE** *enters, snapping their fingers and chanting "prom."* *They pair off and circle each other; the* **BOYS** *all go down on one knee and say "Prom?" and the* **GIRLS** *shout "NO." A final* **ENSEMBLE MEMBER** *blows a whistle and they all exit.*)

Scene 13: Prom-Nope

(**STEPH**, **ADAM**, *and* **TRENT** *at their lunch table.* **TRENT** *is quietly arguing with* **STEPH**. **REINA** *arrives with her lunch.)*

REINA. Hey...

(**TRENT** *gets up and sits at another table.)*

STEPH. Trent is umm...upset.

ADAM. Ooh, trouble in paradise.

REINA. Shut up, Adam.

ADAM. I'm going to tell your mom that you're bullying me.

REINA. Why are you trying to create more drama? Can't you see I already have enough?

ADAM. I do theatre. I live for drama!

Go on...

(*He starts eating popcorn; it could be real or mimed.)*

REINA. *(To* **TRENT**.*)* Trent.

Please don't be mad.

TRENT. You said you liked my design.

REINA. I do.

STEPH. It's a great design. We all agree.

TRENT. Then why are you sneaking around?

Unless you're a liar?

'Cause it sure feels like you've been lying to my face for weeks.

REINA. It's not about the design.

TRENT. Then what?

REINA. ...

TRENT. Then what?!

SPEAK UP.

REINA. I want a date to prom.

TRENT. You want to ditch me and Steph?

REINA. It's not like that.

STEPH. She didn't say that.

TRENT. We've been planning to go together since the beginning of promposals. You said yes!

REINA. I didn't say anything. You just heard yourself so loudly and repeatedly you thought it was my voice.

TRENT. Going to prom with a date is bad for the movement.

ADAM. I definitely have a date.

STEPH. Who?   **TRENT.** I didn't mean you.

ADAM. Emily and Sarah.

It's a show-mance.

But they're double cast.

TRENT. Gross.

ADAM. What can I say? I'm smart, sensitive, and in demand.

STEPH. Or just a straight boy in theatre.

ADAM. Other guys set the bar so low I get to step right over it. Twice.

TRENT. *(To* **REINA.***)* This is exactly the kind of thing we're trying to shut down.

REINA. No, it's not! If they want to go together, they can.

It was the pressure – feeling stuck – feeling like you can't say how you really feel

Because people will be mad or –

REINA. Or worse, because they're just not listening.

TRENT. Who is this perfect prom date? Which of these macho dude bros are you dropping us for?

> (*A song like* "Too Good to Be True"* *starts to play and* **EM** *and some* **ENSEMBLE** *backup dancers enter.* **EM** *sings and hams it up, clearly trying to impress* **REINA**.)

NO.

REINA. How did they know?

STEPH. Umm, I might have mentioned something at the last clinic workshop.

TRENT. I hate Em.

REINA. I don't.

TRENT. Everyone will think you're a sellout.

REINA. Who are these hypothetical people?

TRENT. Me.

EM. Reina, I want to make our prom a night to remember.

STEPH. *High School Musical 3.*

REINA. Did you spill all my guilty pleasures?

STEPH. Everyone loves *High School Musical*!

> (**EM** *and several of the* **ENSEMBLE** *members start to dance.)*

---

* A license to produce *THIS IS NOT A TEEN MOVIE* does not include a performance license for "Too Good to Be True." The publisher and author suggest that the licensee contact ASCAP or BMI to ascertain the music publisher and contact such music publisher to license or acquire permission for performance of the song. If a license or permission is unattainable for "Too Good to Be True," the licensee may not use the song in *THIS IS NOT A TEEN MOVIE* but should create an original composition in a similar style or use a similar song in the public domain. For further information, please see the Music and Third-Party Materials Use Note on page iii.

EM. *(Holding out a big glittery poster.)* Reina, will you go to prom with me?

REINA. I – I –

EM. Reina, I really like you. I think you're smart and funny,

And I love how you're trying to make everything better all the time.

And I want to get dressed up, and dance, and take silly staged pictures together.

REINA. Eh, I – I –

If I go with you, people will think I caved.

That I wasn't serious…

EM. I don't care about other people.

What do you want?

REINA. I, uh, I don't know,

To smash the patriarchy?

Clean water, equal pay, the end of racism, and to live without fear.

EM. Are you afraid of me?

REINA. No. I just don't know how to tell what's real.

> (**REINA** *looks at her friends,* **TRENT**, *and then back to* **EM**.*)*

I can't tell if I want to go with you because *I* want to go with you or if I want to go with you because you just fulfilled this idea of what I thought this moment should be because that's what all the movies and TV and YA novels say it's like.

EM. I'm really confused.

REINA. Me too.

(Her answer.) No.

REINA. I'm sorry.

Please don't be mad.

EM. It's whatever,

I didn't really want to go to prom before anyway.

REINA. Oh, please don't not go because of me!

EM. No offense, but if we're not going together then you don't get to weigh in on my plans.

REINA. Yes, right, sorry.

EM. I hope you figure yourself out.

I'm gonna go.

> (**EM** *exits.*)

REINA. Shit. Shit. SHIT!

Why did I just do that?!

STEPH. Reina, are you…

REINA. *(To* **TRENT.***)* Are you happy now?

> (**REINA** *exits.*)

TRENT. *(Shouting after her.)* No!

Scene 14: Stupid Kids

(Lights shift to a different section of the cafetorium. Projection: U of C slide.)

DR. GRAY. Ethan, we've been meeting for weeks. I need to know, are you ready to make a public apology?

ETHAN. What if I just apologize to Lindsey? Do you think they'd let me come back early?

Coach said if I miss preseason they're going to make me second-string.

DR. GRAY. I wish I could say I cared.

ETHAN. Do you know how much money sports bring to this college? I do, I looked it up. We keep this place going.

DR. GRAY. You want to talk money? OK, how much do you think it costs when the news reports that UC is an unsafe campus, how many students *won't* enroll here, how many families won't pay tuition to send their kids to a college with people like *you*.

ETHAN. This is a waste of time.

*(**ETHAN** starts to exit.)*

DR. GRAY. You need to start talking to your parents about other options. Take a semester off, do credit remediation at community college, transfer.

ETHAN. What? No! You told me that if I take responsibility for my actions, they'd let me back!

Fine! I kissed her without her permission, I should have *asked*. Next time I'll ask! I'll ask!

DR. GRAY. You caused a lot of harm. This isn't a playground. You don't just get a redo, you have to repair and it's clear you're not interested in doing that.

ETHAN. You were never going to help me, you think I'm a bad person.

DR. GRAY. No, Ethan, I don't think you're a bad person, I think you're just a stupid kid.

I think you did something stupid and when someone called you on it, instead of owning it, you did something really mean, which was also stupid. But I don't think you understood the ramifications of your actions because you're a kid, a boy who wasn't taught to think of anything beyond his own self-interest and desires, who felt like his bruised ego was an excuse to make someone else feel afraid. It's frankly childish.

And I do want to help you. I need you to understand *why* what you did was wrong. Not just how to get around the rules and get back to your life as if this never happened, because it did and there is no going back. You did those things and you need to learn from them so you will stop doing stupid stuff that hurts other people. And then I need you tell all your friends who want to EMULATE you, because you're good at kicking or throwing or catching a ball, not to do the same stupid stuff either.

I want to help you, Ethan, I desperately want to help you be a grown-up and not a stupid kid. Because if I don't reach you, and all the other stupid kids like you, you'll just keep hurting people.

So tell me now, are you ready to be an adult and take responsibility for your actions?

> (**ETHAN** *stares at* **DR. GRAY**. *There is no clear indication to his answer; the ambivalence lingers. Lights cross-fade.*)

Scene 15: Getting Ready for Prom Montage!

(Yes, it's the prom montage! The various groups get ready in different areas so that the cast/crew can prep the stage for prom.)

*(***TRENT*** and ***STEPH***. They are both putting on makeup;* ***TRENT*** *keeps checking their phone.)*

STEPH. Has she messaged you?

TRENT. Who?

STEPH. Oh, that's how you're going to play this.

TRENT. No.

Fine.

And, she hasn't posted anything.

She's probably boycotting so she can claim the moral high ground.

STEPH. She's not like judgy like that.

TRENT. She kind of is.

STEPH. No, *you* kind of are.

She just doesn't always push back on what you say.

TRENT. Whose side are you on?

STEPH. Is this middle school?

You had a fight and now you need to work it out.

TRENT. If she apologizes, then I will.

STEPH. Not good enough.

TRENT. This whole no-date thing was her idea!

STEPH. And our prom trio was yours! Even though you knew she's been *obsessed* with having a prom date *forever*!

TRENT. I thought she changed her mind.

STEPH. And she probably thought you'd be chill if she got a date.

TRENT. Well, I'm not!

STEPH. Do you have an enemies-to-lovers fantasy about Em?

TRENT. No!

STEPH. Then what is your deal?

TRENT. She agreed – you were there!

STEPH. No, I believe her.

We both assumed she was on board because she didn't say no.

But you know she wasn't excited.

She didn't contribute to the mood board, she didn't have any color preferences, and she didn't object when you started talking about headpieces, she *hates* headpieces.

TRENT. So what? I'm supposed to apologize because *she didn't* say anything.

STEPH. You're supposed to apologize for assuming without waiting for a real answer.

TRENT. Is this all from your clinic teach-in stuff.

STEPH. *(Kind of surprised.)* Actually, yes it is.

Em isn't so bad, you know.

TRENT. It's not really about Em.

I mean, I don't like them.

Just because we're both nonbinary doesn't mean we have to be best friends.

STEPH. I didn't say that.

TRENT. But everybody acts like it.

"Oh, you're both 'they,' are you all in some club?"

No!

STEPH. OK, but Reina *is* our friend.

And you all can't break up right before college.

I don't have the communication skills to be the go-between and it's going to be hard enough with moving away and not seeing each other every day.

I need us to maintain the group chat and get together on breaks and cheer each other on when things are good and when things are hard.

And you can't ruin that because you're envious that someone asked her to *prom*!

TRENT. OMG! You have our whole lives mapped out!

STEPH. Please! Please! Please!

You need to extend the olive branch!

TRENT. Fine, fine.

I'm coming around,

I just need to make sure I look fabulous before I eat crow.

> (*Lights shift.* **MICHELLE, KAYLA,** *and* **BRITTANY** *in robes with their hair done, doing each other's makeup. They take funny pictures throughout the scene.*)

BRITTANY. You're so good at that!

MICHELLE. Thanks! I'm excited to finally show off my skills!

BRITTANY. How come you don't just wear makeup?

KAYLA. (*Joking.*) Nerd girl rules.

MICHELLE. No! My parents, they have lots of real rules about makeup and clothes and stuff.

KAYLA. I'm just a nerd.

BRITTANY. But you're so pretty.

KAYLA. And smart.

MICHELLE. Just take the compliment!

KAYLA. Fine.

Thanks.

You too.

BRITTANY. I'm glad this is how things turned out.

KAYLA. Me too.

MICHELLE. That's 'cause you didn't want a date to begin with.

KAYLA. That's not the only reason.

MICHELLE. Do you feel weird knowing Adam and Steph staged their rejection?

BRITTANY. I feel kinda dumb that it didn't occur to me that I could say no without them doing that.

MICHELLE. But nobody did!

We were like fish –

Like how fish don't know there's air because they breathe water

It was normal, that's all I'm saying.

BRITTANY. And now, I feel like there's a million other choices out there that I haven't considered.

KAYLA. Yeah...

MICHELLE. And we're about to go to college!

BRITTANY. It's too soon. We just became friends.

KAYLA. We'll stay friends. Michelle and I already have a plan 'cause she's going to State and I'm going to UC.

BRITTANY. I'm going to UC!

KAYLA. Cool.

MICHELLE. Not fair! My mom made me go to State because of that Golden Valley boy who got kicked out of UC. I tried to tell her there are creeps everywhere.

KAYLA. And you basically got a full ride.

MICHELLE. Don't bring facts into this.

KAYLA. You're right, your mom is a big, bad meanie, how dare she make you go to the best premed program in the state!

MICHELLE. Thank you!

I just wish I was going with you and we could take all our classes together and nothing would be different, except the things we want to be different, like boyfriends and parties.

KAYLA. Oh, no thank you to boyfriends and parties!

Besides, we're only going to be two hours away.

BRITTANY. I don't know what I want to major in anymore.

KAYLA. Who says you have to know?

MICHELLE. Parents, teachers, college interview committees, everyone!

BRITTANY. It's so much money, what if I make the wrong decision?

KAYLA. Do you know what makes me mad is that boys get to be dumb and funny and not know. We have to be aware all the time – Is it safe? What does this outfit mean? Am I being too loud? Don't be a stereotype. Don't get taken advantage of. But who is telling the world to look out for us?

That's why I'm going to double major in political science and women and gender studies.

MICHELLE. What! No premed? Since when?

KAYLA. I've been thinking about it for a while.

MICHELLE. And you didn't tell me?

KAYLA. Sometimes I need to have my thoughts in my head for a while before I say them.

MICHELLE. Exactly why you never did Quiz Bowl.

KAYLA. You thought you ate.

MICHELLE. Whatever, you change the sociopolitical structure of the world and I'll hand out the Tylenol.

KAYLA. OK, Dr. Michelle.

MICHELLE. Love you too. UN Ambassador Kayla.

BRITTANY. And me!

Madam CEO of *Teen Vogue*!

KAYLA. Nice!

MICHELLE. Yass!

BRITTANY. Let's go take pictures outside!

> *(Lights shift.* **REINA** *watches* **JACYLN** *get ready. Reina's trio outfit and the dress she picked out for prom are hanging near her.)*

JACYLN. Are you going to get ready?

REINA. I dunno.

> *(***JACYLN*** *continues to get herself ready.)*

Do you *have* to go?!

Can't we just stay home and watch movies together.

Rom-com marathon like when I was little!

Popcorn and swooning, I'll even say yes to *How Stella Got Her Groove Back*.

JACYLN. While I cannot believe I have to pass up my teenage daughter actually asking to spend time with me, not to mention the gorgeous Taye Diggs, I am contractually obligated to chaperone prom.

Don't you want to see the results of your campaign?

REINA. But *everyone* is mad at me.

JACYLN. I think you're being a little –

REINA. Don't you dare say dramatic.

JACYLN. Hyperbolic.

REINA. No!

Maybe.

But it feels so BIG.

It's prom!

That's been the problem this whole time. I want it and I don't and I don't know how to know what *I* want because it's all so – so!

Ugh!

I just want to go back to how it was when I was little – I want to be a kid again.

JACYLN. You're a kid now.

REINA. Mooom!

JACYLN. Honey, Reina, this is just *part* of what your life is going to be, not all of it, not ultimately even the biggest part of it.

Prom is not some self-actualization station where you will suddenly blossom into the next elevated version of yourself. It's not a chrysalis or a Pokémon.

There won't be a big neon sign pointing to your real "major life events." You go through them and only understand how monumental they were when you look back.

REINA. But how am I supposed to know what to do?

And what if I do the wrong thing?

And then everybody is mad at me forever?

REINA. And then I'll never go to college and –

JACYLN. Woo-hoo! Roll that catastrophic thinking back for one second!

Nobody knows what to do all the time.

You just try stuff, and hopefully you learn from it, and then try to do better the next time.

REINA. I wish I could go back and not have done any of this prom stuff.

JACYLN. Well, it's a good thing that a time machine is not on offer because then we wouldn't be instituting our new informed-consent training next semester.

REINA. What! You didn't tell me –

JACYLN. It's not public yet, we're working on solidifying some of the details and figuring out the best way to on board the most reluctant groups.

REINA. Tell them to jump off –

JACYLN. *(Stop.)* Eh-eh! We have to make room for everyone.

REINA. Ugh!

JACYLN. It's progress.

REINA. I guess.

JACYLN. The culture of the school is starting to change, even if it's hard to see right now. You were part of that.

Now, I have to –

REINA. Tell me it's all OK.

JACYLN. It's all OK.

REINA. But, like you mean it.

(**JACYLN** *gives her a look.*)

Please.

JACYLN. Baby, sometimes things suck.
Sometimes you don't like any of your options.
Sometimes you have to make a decision that will upset
someone.
And, even then, it is all OK – even if that person is me,
or your best friends.

I love you,
And I'm proud of you for just being you.

>*(They embrace.)*

REINA. But, what should I do?

JACYLN. Listen to your own little voice and then give
yourself permission to do what you know is right.

I have to go.
I love you no matter what you do.

>*(**JACYLN** exits. **REINA** looks at the outfits,
trying to decide. It is a quiet moment; she
makes a choice. She takes them both offstage.)*

>*(Lights shift. **ALEX** is working on tying a tie or
bow tie. **TERRY** comes in wearing a suit.)*

TERRY. You need help with that?

ALEX. Yeah, my dad never taught me.

TERRY. I got you.

>*(**TERRY** helps **ALEX** tie his tie/bow tie. It's sweet.)*

Dude! You look gooood!

ALEX. Thanks man!

TERRY. Are you ready to bust a move?

>*(He does a flashy dance move or the electric
slide.)*

ALEX. Do you think Jimmy was right?

That girls are just like us.

Well, not *just* like us, but like...

I dunno, just like – once I knew that dates and whatever weren't on the table, it was like I could just talk to them, y'know?

TERRY. Eh, I've been thinking about it and, I think I'm gay.

ALEX. For real?

That's cool.

Good for you, man!

TERRY. But, just to be clear. This is not a date.

ALEX. *(Playfully offended.)* What! How could you resist this hot bod?

TERRY. Bro, duh!

I'm not gay for *you*, no offense.

Just 'cause I'm into guys doesn't mean I'm interested in *every* guy.

ALEX. Dude, I'm just messing with you!

TERRY. We're cool?

ALEX. For sure – just two bros going to prom and one's gay.

> *(Transition to prom. In the original production,* **ALEX** *and* **TERRY** *did a chest bump and yelled "Prom" as they jumped down from the cafetorium stage. The sound/lights switched, and then the rest of the* **ENSEMBLE** *came out in prom outfits and danced a bit.)*

Scene 16: Prom

(The cafetorium, but PROM – there's some decorations and a disco ball, a PROM slide [perhaps cafeteria signs are flipped over to show they're bedazzled on the back]. **REINA** *wears a combination of her thrifted prom dress and her trio outfit, which creates a new look all her own. She stands by a ridiculous poster or decoration.)*

REINA. *(To audience.)* So, this is prom.
It's not what I thought, I don't have a date, I got my own corsage, I parked in my regular parking space and didn't even try to do one of the makeup tutorials Steph sent.

But it's...OK, it's nice,
In a homemade kind of way,
It's nice because of all the effort the student council put in,
And because the teachers are dressed up too,
And because everyone is excited and wants it to be fun, so it is.

And because I came, on my own terms – in my own outfit,
And it feels good because *I* knew I *wanted* to come and I knew it would also be OK if I *didn't* want to.

*(***TRENT*** *and* ***STEPH*** *enter.* ***STEPH*** *waves and then drags* ***TRENT*** *over to* ***REINA***.*)*

STEPH. Can you two please work this out? This is very awkward for me.

REINA. I can do that.

TRENT. Yeah, OK, me too.

REINA. Me first.

I'm sorry I didn't speak up earlier.

REINA. You were so excited, and I kept telling myself I didn't care.

But that wasn't honest.

TRENT. No, I'm sorry I bulldozed you and refused to listen.

And I really don't want to admit this…

STEPH. Do it.

TRENT. But, um, I think the reason I was being so mean about you getting a date.

Is that I was jealous.

STEPH. Envious.

TRENT. Right. Envious.

Not of Em, *ew*.

Sorry!

But that someone was into you like that.

The way they looked at you and all the work they put into that arguably very cringey promposal.

I just want someone to look at me like that.

REINA. They will! You just have to get to college.

You're just in the wrong market.

TRENT. I'm sorry I pressured you not to have a date.

That was your choice to make, not mine.

REINA. It was.

I just didn't feel like I could know what I wanted with any real clarity.

I wasn't even sure if I was going to come.

TRENT. I'm glad you did.

> (*They embrace.* **TRENT** *pulls away and twirls* **REINA**.*)*

And this is a great pastiche! Werk!

STEPH. All is right with the world again!

REINA. As much as it can be until we take down all the oppressive regimes –

STEPH. Topple one thing at a time, comrade!

Tonight we revel!

(They all look around.)

In the cafetorium, with a lot of glitter.

TRENT. You were expecting? Magic?

REINA. At least it smells more like perfume than corn dogs.

STEPH. Did Em come?

REINA. I dunno yet.

Did anyone bring a date?

STEPH. Adam.

> (**ADAM** *waves from a large group of* **GIRLS** *all with matching corsages.)*

REINA. Do you think we really did anything?

STEPH. Brittany got to say no.

TRENT. And look around, no trophy dates, just a bunch of dressed-up doofs in a cafetorium.

> *(An upbeat song starts to play;* * *people start dancing around them.)*

STEPH. Do you want to dance?

---

*A license to produce *THIS IS NOT A TEEN MOVIE* does not include a performance license for any third-party or copyrighted music. Licensees should create an original composition or use music in the public domain. For further information, please see the Music and Third-Party Materials Use Note on page iii.

TRENT. Always!

> *(They begin to dance.)*

REINA. Now?

STEPH. You don't have to if you don't want to.

REINA. Right, right.

> *(She considers.)*

Yes, I do, let's dance!

> *(A big dance number, like all those 90s/2000s teen movies where suddenly everyone knows the moves.)*

End of Play